by

Lori Reid

A is for
Albert

who picks
his nose

(and eats it)

B is for
Betty
who
snoops
on the
neighbors

C is for Cole who doesn't flush the toilet

D is for
Debbie
who eats
with her
mouth
open

E is for
Eli
who butts
in front
of others

F is for
Finn
who slams
the front
door

G is for
Gabriela
who never
says
thank you

To
Gayle
♥
Aunt
Millie

H is for Harry who leaves his dirty dishes on the table

J is for
Jakob
who forces
his farts
out

K is for Kami who thinks she's boss of everyone

M is for
Mallory
who's a
way too
close talker

N is for
Ned
who laughs
at friends
misfortune

O is for Ottis who who spits on the sidewalk

P is for
Patty
who wont
talk
in company

Q is for Quentin

who takes

without

asking

R is for
Ray
who
never
says
sorry

T is for
Tylar
who wont
pull her
pants up

U is for
Uberto
who doesn't
cover his
cough

V is for
Viola
who leaves
her trash
behind

W is for
William
who talks
through
a movie

X is for
Xavier
who cusses
like a
sailor

Y is for
Yun Lee
who primps
at the
table

Z is for

Zak

who chews

his

toenails

Printed in Great Britain
by Amazon